WILLIAM CAREY

HEROES OF THE CROSS

WILLIAM CAREY

MARSHALLS

Marshall Morgan & Scott
1 Bath Street, London EC1V 9LB

Copyright © Marshall Morgan & Scott 1982

First published by Oliphants Ltd 1953
Fifth impression 1962
First issued in paperback in Lakeland 1963

This edition in Marshalls 1982
Impression number 10 9 8 7 6 5 4 3 2 1

ISBN: 0 551 00950 0

Printed in Great Britain by Richard Clay (The Chaucer Press) Ltd,
Bungay, Suffolk

CONTENTS

I

YOUNG WILLIAM

Naturally nobody had a recording machine to preserve William Carey's actual speech—or that of his friends. And if they had, we should find their way of speech old-fashioned and rather stilted. So you'll find in this book only what was actually said, but it's all been interpreted into the sort of speech we use today.

THE little thatched cottage on the edge of the forest should have been perfectly quiet, but it was not. Kindly, weary Mrs. Carey lay listening, half-smiling in the darkness, half anxious. Lively little William Carey lay wide awake because he was talking softly to himself, with his small boy lisp:

"An' two makes six: an' four makes ten: an' eight makes eighteen . . ."

Numbers fascinated him, even although his sixth birthday was a long way ahead: no lullabies would do now for William Carey, no nursery rhymes. ". . . . an' two makes twenty, an' five makes twenty-five . . ."

Suddenly he slept, and the next thing he knew was the cheerful bustle of the early morning. Hurriedly he dressed himself, and out he went into the fresh, bright morning, a sturdy, sprightly little boy.

Nobody knows exactly what he looked like in those days. Cameras had not been thought of or even dreamed about, and cottage weavers earning less than a pound a week between man and wife were not in the habit of having their children's portraits painted. And anyway it is to be doubted if young William could have endured more than a five-minute sitting, even if any one had wished to paint him for nothing!

What we do know is largely guess work, founded on facts. Certainly his eyes were large and brown: almost certainly his skin was pale and clear. And it is most likely that he had everyday brown hair to go with them, for had he been ginger or unusually fair, it would hardly have escaped comment. We cannot tell, and we have no way of telling, for William was seriously ill when he was quite a young man, and he lost all his hair; from then on he wore a wig—and a very ungainly and badly made wig it was.

This brown-eyed child was small for his age, and as far as we can judge from the shape of his face in later portraits, he probably had a wide forehead and a little pointed chin in childhood. We shall not say too much about his nose, because though this was straight enough, I doubt if it was ever a *little* nose.

The same nose twitched at the good breakfast smells which soon came from the cottage kitchen, and he was quickly indoors and disposing of a hearty, though very plain breakfast.

By the time breakfast was over his father was already busy at his loom. "Clacketty-clack! Clacketty-clack!" it went, on and on, apparently

endlessly. But William was so used to the noise
that he hardly heard it. He had his own duties
to perform while the womenfolk—grandmother,
mother, and even tiny four-year-old sister Ann—
were busy over the breakfast things. There was
wood to find in the forest, there was water to
fetch—and there were all the fascinations of
growing and living things out of doors to make the
tasks take a good long time.

But once he had finished William came straight
in to join Ann and grandmother in the back
kitchen for lessons. Of course William knew his
letters by now, and so when they had said their
catechism Ann was set to making pot-hooks on
the old, worn slate, while William sat close to
grandmother, learning, sometimes to read, sometimes the multiplication tables, and sometimes to
master the fascinating mysteries of "taking away."

He enjoyed his lessons with grandmother.
Occasionally his father would teach him a little,
when he was not too busy at the weaving. But his
father was strict, and a bit solemn, and it was hard
work to get a word of praise out of him. Grandmother was gentle, and encouraging; and she
never snapped. To learn with her was sheer
delight.

William loved her stories too. He liked to hear
her talking about "my own little William": she
had lost him when he was a fine grown lad,
already teaching in a village school near their
home . . . and grandfather Carey had died in the
same year.

Grandmother's gentle face would grow sad and wistful as she talked about them; but then she would look into the loving, pitying face of this younger William, and her eyes would brighten.

"And you, William, are named after him!" she would say. "Your dear father and mother let me choose your name: and they named your little sister after me, too! What do you think of *that*?"

William did not think a great deal of that, except perhaps to say to himself that if grandmother had not lived with them little sister might have been named after mother: and Ann was an easier name than Elizabeth!

Above all he liked to hear about grandmother's other son, Uncle Peter. William was something of an adventurer himself, though he was so young; and it excited him to hear of the uncle who went as a lad to Canada. Sometimes grandmother's tones were sad as she talked of him, because she hardly dared hope to see him again. No letters came, and people who have had great sorrows find it painfully easy to fear the worst, when they have no word from their loved ones.

As it happened, Uncle Peter did come back to England, and a great help he was to William. But whether he came in time for grandmother to see him we do not know. A little while before William's sixth birthday came round, grandmother died, and a sore loss it was to the lively, affectionate little boy.

Ann was too young to remember for long, but William carried an aching heart about with him for many a day, and for many a long night shed tears into his pillow, instead of "casting accompts" as his mother described his bedtime arithmetic.

Happily at this time there came a great change for the whole family. Until he died Grandfather Carey had been a person of some eminence in Paulerspury, where they lived—a straggling Northamptonshire village of thatched cottages, with its village inn, the free school, the impressive rectory, and a sturdily built church.

Grandfather Carey had been the parish clerk and the master of the free school, where those who wished—or those whose parents wished—learned reading, writing, mathematics and Latin. Of course it was a church school, and there was much learning of the catechism, and a good deal of religious teaching. In fact, only the children of parents who belonged to the Church of England could attend: chapel folk, "dissenters" they were called, were not allowed to send their children. But then nearly everyone in Paulerspury held a very poor opinion of the dissenters.

Now the man who had filled the post after grandfather Carey, had gone; and William's father, Edmund Carey, was offered the post. He accepted it, and then came all the excitement of a move to the other end of the village.

The house was a doll's house of a place, with two windows on either side of the little front door, with its round stone doorstep; and two windows above those. There were two chimneys, one at each end of the thatched roof, and in front of the

house, two plane trees which through the winter
months dangled their blackish bobbles from every
branch.

At the side of the house was the school building,
also thatched, looking rather like a miniature
barn, with a tiny diamond-paned window on
either side of the door.

I expect William and Ann peeped in fascinated
awe into that hall of learning. It was no luxurious
place. Wooden beams supported the roof: the
walls were whitewashed. Tree-trunks split in half,
with crude legs thrust into holes bored in the
rounded sides, made benches for the scholars.
The schoolmaster was the only person to have a
desk. And near to his hand there would be the
birch-rod for the rebellious and the tall dunce's
cap for the stupid.

To William the supreme advantage of the
school house itself lay in one fact: he was able to
have a room all to himself. To us nowadays that
is no uncommon thing: but to an eighteenth
century village boy of only six years, it was a
peerless privilege.

Behind the school house was a garden, and
better still, a fruitful orchard. But best of all, at
the bottom of the garden, separating the school
house land from that of the rectory, was a narrow
moat.

Oh, the delights of that stretch of water, shaded
in spring and summer by a fairyland of trees! It
had a mystery about its shadowy coolness, a
beauty which the little Careys were still too

young to realise to the full, though they could not help being influenced by it. And, to descend to a more mundane level, the water swarmed with tadpoles, sticklebacks, and a variety of small fishes.

One more joy the school house had: its nearness to the stage-coach rôutes, so that a run of a few hundred yards brought William to the place where he could watch the London to Liverpool stage-coach go by: where an occasional horseman would canter past, and twice a week great wheeled wagons, drawn by six or eight horses, would lumber along, carrying goods from London into Lancashire and Cheshire.

In the midst of all these pleasures William soon forgot his grief, and only happy memories of his grandmother remained. Life was too full for repining. There were the inevitable home duties, and now there were also lessons in school, and the multitude of doings which occupied the spare time of the little group of schoolboys.

William was soon well to the fore among them. He was always small for his age, but he was sturdy and daring, always on the move. Whatever he did, he did with his whole heart. In school he worked with a will, and he stuck at any subject he tackled until he had mastered it.

Out of school he was something of a ringleader, and nothing daunted him. His pluck was the talk of his school-fellows. For instance, there was one tree in Paulerspury which no one could climb, and the thought of it tantalised young William unbearably. At last one day he exclaimed:

"Come on! *I'm going up that tree!*"

With understandable anxiety his friends watched him as he worked his way agilely upward from branch to branch. Then there was a gasp of horror, for down he came, crashing heavily downward from branch to branch. Head over heels he came, landing on the ground with a terrible thump.

They rushed to help him to his feet, profoundly relieved to find that he could stand. But poor William's place on the wooden bench was empty for quite a few days.

When he did return to school it was to mutter to his cronies, "*I did it!*"

"What d'you *mean?*" they gasped.

"Waited till mother was out of the way yesterday, and slipped out. And I got right up to the top!" It was not that William was over-boastful it was just that he had set himself to conquer an obstacle, and it had to be done. The fact that it cost him an awful effort, undertaken with aching bruises and trembling limbs, was just beside the point.

He showed the same courage over his toothache. Village boys in the eighteenth century could not go into a telephone call-box and make an appointment with the dentist when they had toothache. Toothache either had to be put up with, or someone had to get the tooth out somehow.

William's "somehow" was ingenious, if crude. He enlisted the aid of one of his friends, who was stationed beside a large grinding wheel. Tied to the wheel was a piece of string: the other end of the string was persuaded around the offending tooth.

"Wait till I say 'Go'!" William ordered.

Then he took his stand, crossed his arms, called up all his courage, and shouted, "Go!"

The boy at the wheel gave a mighty turn—and we shall never know whether or not William gave a mighty yell. But he felt and resisted a mighty tug, and endured a mighty wrenching, and it was out.

At least he felt no more toothache!

The school-house was well filled by this time. William and Ann were joined by the babies, Mary and Tom, and later there came, too, a child from the village. She was an orphan who had no one at all to care for her; and because Edmund Carey never forgot the kindness he and his mother had received from the villagers when she was left a widow, and he was only seven, he and his wife gave the little one a home until she was old enough to keep herself. So there were seven of them to feed and clothe.

Mrs. Carey at times found it very hard to make ends meet. Happily vegetables were plentiful and cheap, and clothes were mostly home made. People were amused with simple things in those days, and did not demand the luxuries we take for granted. Certainly William's life was far from dull.

He loved nothing better than to wander alone through woods and fields in a never-ending search for treasures. Plants, insects, birds and their nests, unusual stones—anything was welcome for his collection. It may be that it was as well that he *had* his own precious little room to himself, for few would have cared to sleep in the same quarters as some of his specimens. He liked them alive better than dead, insects and fishes as well as birds, and they were in every corner of the room.

Ann did not seem to share these interests, but when his second sister, Mary—known to the family and to us as Polly—grew old enough, she was his eager and interested companion.

When Polly was a grown woman she still remembered her jaunts with her big brother, through woods and fields, wet grass and muddy stretches, sometimes fiercely "hushed" no doubt, but always carefully taught concerning the interests and beauties of growing things.

She found William's room fascinating: it was a veritable museum, aviary, aquarium and insectarium. The birds throve, or did not thrive: and sometimes Polly earned bitter reproaches when she overfed them, and they were later found dead. But William was always forgiving, and never discharged his willing helper.

Perhaps the least that is said about the odours which proceeded from his fish tanks the better! The insects were kept in restraint—with more or less success—and their development was watched and recorded with passionate interest.

William soon found that if he wanted to keep a

proper record of their habits he must learn to draw. He also taught himself to paint with some skill, and it was not long before he had earned quite a reputation as a naturalist in the village. If anyone found an unknown flower, bird or insect, they were advised: "Tek it to Bill Carey: he'll tell you all about it."

Even baby Tom was taken on nature-hunts, and the small-for-his-age William would carry the bouncing two-year-old in his arms on his walks, pointing out to the baby all the loveliness of growing wild things.

Uncle Peter was a great help in this hobby of his. When he came back to England he settled in Paulerspury as a gardener. Uncle Peter was childless, and he took a fatherly interest in this eager young nephew.

Soon after the family had moved to the schoolhouse he began to teach him how to cultivate garden flowers, and before long William was put in charge of the schoolhouse garden. He never lost his joy in flowers and trees—and we shall hear more of this love of his.

He enjoyed Uncle Peter's company for other things, beside himself and his gardening lore. By the hour he would listen enthralled to stories of foreign parts, of the voyage over the great sea; Indians in Canada, of the French, of blazing summers and brilliant autumns, and snowy winters; of waterfalls and lakes, rivers and rapids, until his heart burned with longing to see the great world. There was something of a wanderlust in the Carey family, and young William had more than his fair share of it.

But even school, play, nature study, gardening, were not all of William's life. In every spare moment he had his nose in a book: he was a voracious reader. He did not read many story-books, for there were none particularly readable for boys in those days: but scientific, historical and travel books he loved. He could not buy many, but he was a champion borrower!

The *Life of Columbus* held him utterly enthralled, and finally his schoolfellows grew so weary of hearing of the great traveller that they nick-named his admirer "Columbus."

Religious books Carey did *not* like—in fact he actively disliked them, save only for *The Pilgrim's Progress*, and that he read for its story, and not for what it taught.

William was taken to church from an early age, and after he had joined the school he used to sit in a row with the other boys, on Sunday, instead of in the pew with the family, directly under the eye of his parish-clerk-cum-school-master father. So he could not help learning a good deal about religion, and he learned more at home, where he was thoroughly taught *about* the Bible. When he grew older he was to be thankful for that careful teaching, but at the time it reached as far as his mind, and not a whit farther.

II

THE BREADWINNER

WILLIAM gazed out of the tiny windows of the schoolroom at the brilliant fields, which were divided into little diamonds by the leaded panes. The fields, the growing things . . . soon they would be all his life.

It was not that he disliked his lessons: he had always been a keen worker, and at twelve had been the talk of the school for the ardour with which he learnt nearly the whole of a Latin Vocabulary!

He did not find it hard to attend, and his present day-dreaming was a most unusual thing. But when you are fourteen, and within a few days of your first job, a job which is to bring in a whole five shillings a week—and five shillings went a mighty long way in those days—well, it was enough to take any boy's mind off his lessons.

What William did not realise was the sort of life it would be. His imagination was so filled with the idea of being a man and a breadwinner, dealing all the time with things he could grow, that he forgot what long hours in the fields—from dawn till sundown and perhaps later—would mean.

William loved to read: he was fascinated by study. It did not occur to him that his new life would leave no energy for books; that at the end of a day's field work he would be ready to eat, to doze off in a chair, and then reel up to his bed to sleep again, dreamlessly, till he must drag himself from his bed again in the early dawn. *And you can't read a book while you're tilling the ground.*

Whether he enjoyed his farmer's boy life or not, we have never been told, nor how much his museum and his living plants and creatures suffered by his absence all day: though no doubt faithful Polly did her best to help him.

But God wanted William Carey for something better than land work, and God used one of the everyday facts of his life to lead him to something better.

Ever since he was seven William had had a lot of trouble with his skin. It wasn't that he had sores, or roughness, or anything that could be seen—or hardly ever. But he just could not stand the sunlight. After the first hot, sunny spell in his new job, he went to bed night after night in agony. His hands and face were so painful that they kept him awake nearly all night, every night, and no ointment or potion or lotion his mother could produce did any good. Nothing relieved him.

There were no skin specialists for village boys in those days, and so William went through that first summer bearing his sufferings as well as he could, worn out with pain, and sleeplessness, and hard, long hours of heavy work. Oh, the relief of the dull winter days! The hardship of turning out on bitter, dark mornings was nothing compared with what he had been through, and he could at least sleep.

His parents had watched him with painful anxiety, and after the second summer had passed they decided to put him to some other work, before the next year's hot weather came round.

There were other reasons, too, why they felt he should have a change. The boy was friendly with a most undesirable group of village lads, who used to foregather with the heroes of the local football team at the village blacksmith's shop. And soon he was one with them in swearing, lying, and the type of unpleasant talking-in-corners which horrified his mother and sisters. Finally his father forbade him to go there.

Then there were scenes at home, with an angry father demanding: "Have you been to the black-smith's again, my son?" and a slight, brown-eyed William looking him straight in the face and saying, "No, father, honestly I haven't!"

Then the father would show William that he knew that he *had* been there again, and had added lies to disobedience. And there would be trouble which clouded the happiness of the home. At such times Edmund Carey was very stern; but he was a kindly parent, and what he could do for his son he did.

Before the next hot weather came round, when William was sixteen, he left home as a shoe-maker's apprentice. Nine miles north-east of Paulerspury, over the newly cut canal, was Piddington. The shoemaker there had lost his apprentice: the boy had run away, and even a full description of his person and his clothing, published in the *Northampton Mercury*, had failed to trace him.

So the shoemaker, Clarke Nichols by name, took on two more apprentices: first John Warr, a lad from Potterspury, near William's own village, and a little later William Carey. The two villages were only a few miles apart, so it may well be that the two boys already knew each other, which would take the edge off William's first loneliness.

There had been loving farewells and much good counsel before he set out, with a stick in his hand and his clothes in a bundle; and he tramped through the well-known lanes with a tender heart and a head full of good resolutions.

The life was interesting: there was much to learn. Leather must be prepared, and William must make acquaintance with a multitude of tools before he could be trusted to cut the welts and uppers, the soles and heels. And William was always a good learner.

John Warr was three years his senior, and being a good-natured youth he helped him in learning his new tasks—the more so because his grandfather and father had been shoemakers, and it was not all new and strange to him.

Clarke Nichols was a staunch churchman, which was probably one reason why Edmund Carey was ready to trust him with his son. What Edmund Carey did not know was that Nichols's churchmanship was a matter of outward appearances: the plain truth was that he was a heavy drinker, and cared so little for the Lord's day that his apprentices were kept at work delivering shoes right up till church time.

He had a hot temper and a scathing tongue: but he had one virtue which William sadly lacked—a blessed regard for truth. *He loathed a lie.* He was the right man for sixteen-year-old William Carey in that respect at least.

But if Clarke Nichols's churchmanship did not have much effect on his daily life, he dearly loved an argument about religion, and he and William joined in furious heckling of John Warr, who went to chapel—a dissenter!

As a matter of fact John's chapel views at that time made no more difference to his daily life than Clarke Nichols's and William Carey's church views. But the three had many wordy battles, and William was clever enough to come off verbal victor four times out of five. Though he admitted in later life that he often knew he was not honestly in the right.

Arguments sometimes are worthless: but in this case they were to have good results. John Warr, who was busy arguing against Christian cere-monies which were allowed to take the place of Christian experience, began to realise that his own sins had never been dealt with, that the Lord Jesus Christ—who was only too willing to make a new man of him—had precious little hold on his life. And so John began to think, with his heart as well as with his mind.

And the more he became convinced that he

needed a Saviour, the more eagerly he pleaded with William. And through his pleading with William he himself became a true Christian in the end.

William could soon see that John's life was different: you don't set yourself to thinking seriously about spiritual things without its having some effect on your daily living.

So William grew uneasy. He knew well enough what his own life was, and the time came when he was brought near to hating himself.

III

THE ERRING APPRENTICE

IT was one Christmas time, and William set out to fulfil a very pleasant duty, in addition to the jobs he had to do for his master.

According to custom he was to call on all the shopkeepers and other people with whom Clarke Nichols did business, to collect Christmas boxes. And on the way home William was going to do some shopping of his own. He never told what he had planned to buy: but I think there must have been useful gifts for his father and mother, ribbons for his sisters, and something good to eat for young Thomas, who still had not reached his teens.

One of his calls was at the ironmonger's.

"Happy Christmas, sir!" William said, as he turned to go, when the business was done—hoping, of course, to be called back.

"Happy Christmas, lad!" responded Mr. Hall. "Ah! wait a moment. Don't forget your Christmas box. Listen, lad, which will ye have, a sixpence, or a shillun'?"

William's brown eyes were turned in puzzlement upon the man. He was not a pleasant man, and William would have said that a shilling far exceeded the bounds of *his* generosity. But William was a boy, and he said what we'd have said.

"Shilling, please, sir, and thank you kindly!" and away he went with a heart full of pleasure.

Other people were generous that day, and William began his shopping, But when he had nearly finished he discovered the reason for the ironmonger's generosity: the shilling was a brass one, false coinage.

William's eyes sparkled in anger: it was a mean trick, and what was he to do? For the worst part of it all was that he had, in a sense, already spent part of that shilling. He had some of Clarke Nichols's money jumbled up with his own in his pocket, and unless he gave his master the bad coin, there would not be enough change, and there was going to be trouble.

There are always two ways of meeting trouble: to take what's coming to you like a man, or to try to lie your way out of it. William decided to lie. But he did more than that: all the way home he had the impudence to pray earnestly that God would help him to pull the wool over his master's eyes.

"Let him believe it, Lord, and I'll be a better chap for the rest of my days!" Something like that, William's prayer went. It was a very earnest prayer, but it was a prayer that a holy God would help him in telling a lie, and help him to pass off a false coin as a true one.

No one will ever write better of what God *did* do than William Carey himself wrote, years afterwards: "A gracious God did *not* get me safe through!"

There was a fine rumpus when William tried to put his plan into effect.

"Hey! this shilling's a bad one, my lad. What's the meaning of this?" demanded Clarke Nichols.

William was an experienced liar, but still he was not a very efficient one. His shamed face made his master suspicious.

"Hey, you there, Warr!" he shouted. "Get over to Mr. Hall the ironmonger's, and find out if he's given young Carey here a bad shilling!"

William waited in shame and agony. Clarke Nichols waited in rising anger. And at last John Warr came back with the true facts—and we'll give him the credit of believing that he came back very reluctantly.

William wished the ground would open and swallow him up: he had to put up with much hearty and well-deserved abuse before the matter was allowed to rest. And even then he felt bitterly ashamed and humiliated: he hated himself.

It took weeks to convince him that the story was not all over Piddington, and he would not set foot in the church—in fact he would hardly go out at all—until he was sure that the thing was not being talked about.

The religious arguments still went on over the shoemaking, and William's attitude gradually began to change. It was perfectly true what John Warr said, that so far his churchmanship and his Christian training had not prevented him from doing all sorts of things which were utterly unworthy of his church . . . William grew more uneasy. He must be a *better* churchman. He would go there three times every Sunday.

And he did: and was perhaps in danger of turning into a first-class prig. But what was more important, John Warr persuaded him to go to his own little meeting house. William did not go there on Sundays, of course: church loyalty forbade it. But there was a prayer meeting in the week to which he went: and sometimes when he was alone he even tried to pray in secret. For very shame he began to fight against his habit of lying, and because swearing was not in keeping with all the rest, he began to watch his tongue, too.

Something else helped. Being William he had long ago investigated all the books in his master's house. Some of them meant little to him: he still held to his early distaste for religious books.

Only one of these, by Jeremy Taylor, awoke in him great longings after a better way of life.

But one volume claimed his full attention, and he would not rest until he had mastered it. On the outside cover were the words "New Testament Commentary," and William's familiarity with the Bible was of the type which breeds contempt. But idly glancing through the book he saw strange characters in an unknown tongue.

Immediately he took it to Clarke Nichols. "What's all this mean, sir? What language is it? Do you know it?"

"Greek, I believe," was the laconic reply. "And it's Greek to me. Scholar's stuff, that is. Leave it be, boy!"

But the boy had no intention of leaving it be. He began to make his plans. At home in Paulerspury was a weaver, Thomas Jones, who had been well educated. He was poor now, and ill thought of, for his poverty was the result of his own evil living.

William cared nothing for that. On his very next visit home he called on Jones, rather shyly, and with something of awe at the man who had been so very bad, and made his request.

"Mr. Jones, I found this book at Mr. Nichols's. He says it's Greek. It just fascinates me, and I'd give anything to read it. *Please* can you help me?"

The worn and rather coarsened scholar looked at the slight, eager boy; and it may be that he felt shame at that moment, remembering what he himself had once been. Once he had thirsted for knowledge, but now . . .

"I'm rusty," he answered slowly. "It's years since I looked at a bit o' Greek. But I'll do what I can . . ."

I believe Thomas Jones looked forward as eagerly as William did to the boy's monthly visits home. Soon he had bought a Greek glossary and grammar to polish up his own knowledge, but even that polishing up process did not prevent his scholar from outstripping him, so that in a surprisingly short time the shoemaker's apprentice knew two classical languages—Greek as well as Latin. Certainly God was preparing William Carey for an out-of-the-ordinary life work.

The wise people who know Greek tell us that it

enriches the reading of the New Testament beyond dreams. And these riches, with John Warr's persuasions, and the tenderness of William's conscience after the disastrous episode of the shilling, led him by degrees to accept the new life which the Lord Jesus Christ alone can give. He never knew the actual date of his conversion, but he was in no doubt about the fact of it.

Sunday church-services and week-day chapel prayer-meetings had a new meaning. But one Sunday when William was eighteen something happened which was to prove vitally important in his life.

It was a national day of prayer, and Sunday though it was, William spent that day at the chapel. And the things he heard made him feel quite certain that his place was with the despised chapel folk, from then on. It was two years before he formally joined himself to the dissenters, but after that day of prayer William stood with them.

Nobody knows exactly what the loyal churchman, Clarke Nichols, thought about this step, which in those days was almost a matter for scandal. For in the same year he died. But he could not have felt too badly about it, for before he died he himself came to trust in the Lord Jesus Christ as his Saviour, chiefly because the way the two young apprentices lived in his house now, made it plain just what salvation really meant.

It would be nice to write of a life-long friendship between William Carey and John Warr, even after Clarke Nichols's death sent them on their separate ways. In actual fact we know nothing more at all about John's life—except this: I am quite certain that in heaven he and William Carey have many a happy talk about old days in Piddington.

IV

THE FAMILY MAN

WILLIAM had to find himself a new job. He had not quite finished his training before Nichols died, but he knew enough about his trade to be a useful helper.

Not very far away from his home was Hackleton, where the shoemaker, Mr. Thomas Old, was needing help: probably he was not sorry to have William to work for him, for he didn't have to pay such high wages to a young man who was not fully experienced.

But William was already a skilful worker, and before he had worked long for Mr. Old one of the pairs of shoes he made so pleased his employer that his verdict was: "*These* stay in the shop, just to show our customers the sort of work we turn out!" And stay they did.

Once he had settled down in Hackleton William went with Mr. and Mrs. Old to the little meeting house there: Mr. Plackett, Mrs. Old's father, was one of the leaders of the chapel, and soon William came to know him, and his daughter Dorothy.

Soon Dorothy began to occupy a special place in William's thoughts and in his heart. Small-for-his-age William Carey was old for his years, so it did not matter a bit that Dorothy was five years older than he was. He loved her, and that was what mattered. It did not matter a bit that she had spent all her life in a village without a school, and that nobody had bothered to teach a girl to read.

At their wedding she made her mark in the marriage register with a large, rather wobbly cross: but the curate who performed the ceremony was very little better off, for the best he could do with the spelling of her name was "Dority"; her bridesmaid sister Lucy was "Lusie," and the other sister, Catherine, was "Katran"!

William was happy in his little cottage home. He and Dorothy loved one another tenderly, and it was delightful to have a home all of his own, after living for years in other people's houses. It was a busy life: there was his job to be done, language study to keep up, meetings to attend, his garden to make and care for, until it was a glory of flowers; and soon a new task.

The year that he married William was accepted into membership of the Hackleton meeting house, and one eventful day "Brother Carey" was asked to speak a few words on the Scripture reading. We can only too well imagine the beating heart, the hot hands, the dry throat of which William was so painfully conscious as he stood up to speak. But he did speak, and the people liked what he had to say.

Soon he was invited to other places to preach, and when some people from another village in Carey's part of the country, called Earls Barton, met him at a Baptist Association meeting, they asked him to speak at their chapel.

That Baptist Association meeting was important for another reason: there Carey met the three men who were to be lifelong friends of his: John Sutcliff, John Ryland, and Andrew Fuller—and these are names to remember.

No sooner had the Earls Barton chapel people heard Carey than they asked him to preach for them regularly, once a fortnight: and for three years, some of them marked by sorrow and illness, William tramped the long six miles every other Sunday morning, returning at night to his cottage.

Of course he did not know it at the time, but this preaching—which earned him nothing and cost him a good deal of energy and shoe leather, and wear and tear of clothing—was a new kind of apprenticeship.

The Paulerspury chapel folk soon heard of it, and somewhat to Edmund Carey's embarrassment, they asked William to preach to them. Of course the family knew all about his chapel-going, and they put up with it very well, really, especially as he was far too enthusiastic to be tactful. He argued endlessly with them, trying to get them to leave the Church of England, and he was none too polite about it.

But Edmund Carey was still parish clerk, and master of a school where dissenters' children might not attend! Yet he was patient with his son's enthusiasm, and even allowed him to conduct family prayers when he did come home. Sometimes in so doing William made his devoted Polly, now a young woman, inwardly furious.

"We know, Lord," he would pray, "that all our righteousnesses are as filthy rags . . ."

And angry Polly would think to herself: "He doesn't think *his* righteousness is so: it's me and the family he looks on as 'filthy' . . ." But Polly loved William too much to quarrel with him, and the day was to come when she, and Ann too, were to love the Lord as he did.

It was a good thing that there was no quarrel with home, for before long William and his Dorothy were needing all the loving help they could get.

They were still happy in their little cottage, with a baby daughter to add to their joy, when Mr. Old died. William took over the business, and erected his own sign outside—doubtless with some inward pride. But trouble soon came. One of the most important of Mr. Old's customers cancelled a very big order, and that meant that all those boots and shoes must be re-sold before more could be made: for there was no money for fresh leather.

Mid-England had not known such a severe winter as that one for years and years: and trade was bad all over the country. But William must spend the cold months tramping through snow and wind and rain, from village to village, trying to get rid of the apparently inexhaustible supply of boots and shoes left on his hands.

He and Dorothy could *not* make ends meet: some days they quite literally went hungry. At last in desperation, as if he had not work enough to do already, William opened a little evening school which brought in a few shillings a week.

So that his days were taken up with shoe-making with a book at hand, and with tramping the countryside: his evenings in teaching raw country boys: and half his nights in the one thing which never failed to claim his absorbed interest, his language study. And when he had an idle moment, there was the delightful baby to be played with, and of course the garden must continue to be neat and well filled.

His family in Paulerspury had no idea of what was going on. William said nothing about it when he went home, and since he was still tramping every other week to Earls Barton, as well as preaching in the home village, they took it for granted he was managing to keep going fairly well.

But there was hunger in his little cottage, and later there was sickness, sad, desperate sickness: and the day came when William and Dorothy lost their baby daughter.

This blow was too bitter: soon William himself was desperately ill, and at last poor Dorothy, heartbroken as she was at the loss of her baby, sent to Paulerspury for help.

When William's mother arrived at the little cottage—and she arrived very promptly—she was horrified to find the state in which they were living: to think that her boy should actually be going hungry!

But there was no time for wondering and questioning. Speedily she settled in to nurse him.

and to comfort and help poor bereft Dorothy. And how grateful they were for her help! But the thing which touched William most, when he was well enough to hear about it, was what his young brother Thomas did.

Thomas was still only fifteen, probably just beginning to earn his own living. But that loyal, generous boy sold all his treasures—at least all that anyone would buy—and added the sum to his savings; and he handed the lot over to help William out of his troubles.

Gradually William responded to his mother's nursing and care, until he was well enough for her to leave them again. At last he got back to his work, and spent long hours bending over the leather which seemed so stiff and hard in his trembling hands.

Wearily he dragged over the long miles, selling his shoes and bringing home fresh leather: he had a boy to help him now, but Parker was young, and poor sick, irritable William was so far from being his usual sunny self that one day when the boy let the wax boil all over the stove, he flicked him sharply with his stiff leather apron. Parker was not pleased *then*, but the day was to come when he would boast of that bit of weary irritability.

Still, William Carey never lost the pluck which marked his boyhood. When he was actually ill in bed he could do nothing but pray for the people in Earls Barton: but as soon as he could stand on his feet again he tramped those long six miles there and back again, ignoring shaking knees and a racking cough—and one other embarrassing discomfort. For after his fever was better he went quite bald—and the only wig he could afford was a very badly made, ill-fitting and unbecoming affair. And imagine tramping six miles in a high wind with a wig under your hat!

Something else happened during that time, something very important. One October Sunday at daybreak he left home to walk the five miles to Northampton. There, at six o'clock in the cold morning light, in the cold water of the river Nen, William Carey was baptised.

He was the only one to be baptised that day: there was no crowd of people, and no one there realised what he was going to be and to do. They saw just a poor, shabby, insignificant little brown-eyed shoemaker, who had to remove a badly-fitting wig before the ceremony in which he bore witness to the fact that Jesus Christ was his Saviour and his Lord.

V

"BEE IN HIS BONNET"

IF you were poor you could not live just where you liked in William Carey's days. So that when twenty-four years old William heard that a schoolmaster was wanted in Moulton, five miles beyond Earls Barton, he could not simply find a house and move in to take over the new job, just because it would mean a little more money to keep himself and his wife.

No. First he had to get a certificate signed by three important people from Paulerspury, stating that it was his home village. Then his parents must add their signatures, and then two magistrates theirs. Armed with this document he must go to the village leaders in Moulton, and only then did he receive permission to settle in their village.

They found a cottage on the outskirts of the village—a tiny thatched place it was, in the middle of a short row of six. Moving was not a very complicated business: their poverty meant that they had very little furniture. So that soon the house was shipshape, and William turned his attention to the garden. In the garden were the ruins of an old outhouse, which had to be pulled down and cleared away, before he could begin to plant anything. But it was not long before hard work and his "green fingers" had turned that little patch of land into a place his soul could rejoice in.

Once the school was opened pupils soon came, though William was not such a good schoolmaster as his father was, if Polly is to be believed. She seemed to think that he was not a very good disciplinarian!

But he was an exciting geography teacher. He loved the subject, and he taught it well; and quite certainly there was not a boy in his school who would not have given all his meagre possessions in exchange for Master Carey's globe—though *not* for the purpose of learning geography.

William could not afford to buy one of the newfangled globes the shops were selling. But he could make one. And after a certain amount of thinking and planning, and it may be a bit of help from Dorothy, he cut out of leather and stitched together and stuffed what looked like a perfect football.

But this ball was not to be kicked. Soon the seas and continents and islands were drawn in and coloured: and William's pupils learned about the countries of the world with inward hankerings after a game of football on the green over the road!

It was while he was school-mastering in Moulton that he became a member of the Baptist denomination. And when the Baptist chapel in the village asked him to become their pastor, he gladly agreed. His three friends with the names to be remembered—John Sutcliff, John Ryland, and Andrew Fuller—were all there at his ordination.

Moulton chapel was a tiny, dilapidated place, and the people were poor, so William's salary was a very small one. Certainly it was not enough, even with what the school brought in, to keep William, Dorothy, and the three little boys who arrived, one after the other, to fill the lonely places in Dorothy's heart.

Before long William was shoe-making again, this time working for a man named Thomas Gotch, whose name is worth remembering if only for one kindness. It so happened that Andrew Fuller had been to visit William, and he went back to his home in Kettering deeply impressed by the way he lived. He told this Thomas Gotch, who was one of the deacons at his own church, all about the life of this pastor-schoolmaster-shoemaker he employed, who did so much work, and still found time to keep a lovely garden.

The next time William took a bagful of finished shoes to Mr. Gotch, his employer gave him a quizzical look.

"Let me see, Mr. Carey," he said thoughtfully. "How much a week do you earn by your shoe-making?"

"About nine or ten shillings, sir," answered William slowly, in some perplexity.

Gotch's eyes twinkled: "Well, now, I've a secret for you. *I don't mean you to spoil any more of my leather!*"

William gasped. Was this dismissal? He had always put his best into Mr. Gotch's work, and he had never *said* he was not satisfied . . .

But Mr. Gotch soon put his mind at rest, and told him something which filled his heart with thankfulness:

"Get on as fast as you can with your Latin and Hebrew and Greek," he said kindly. "And I'll allow you ten shillings a week from my private purse!"

So back home he went to study and study and study, with more ardour than ever. Before long he had started on French and Dutch and Italian, as well as getting on with Greek and Hebrew and Latin. He was insatiable!

Still he tramped mile after mile to preach; still he taught in his school, and found time to teach his little sons.

It was a full life, but although it was an obscure one, too, William's adventuring soul was not altogether tied down to the tiny Northamptonshire village. He had an intense interest in what was happening all over the world.

At about this time a very expensive book was published, and oh, how William would have loved to buy it! But he did manage to borrow a copy—all his friends were wonderfully kind about getting hold of books for him. It was *The Last Voyage of Captain Cook*, and as Carey read of new lands and strange peoples he thrilled with interest.

Captain Cook had no idea of taking the Gospel to these heathen of the Pacific Islands: cynically enough he said that neither fame nor profit would

drive anyone to attempt to introduce Christianity
there.

But Carey had long been concerned about the
needs of the untaught heathen, and as he read
of dark-skinned men in canoes swarming around
Cook's ships *Resolution* and *Discovery*, of landings
on coral beaches where the people might be
friendly or might be cannibals, he was entranced
with the adventure; but his heart burned with the
longing to take the Gospel to them.

In those days Christian people in Britain
seemed to feel that there was so much work to
be done in England, in preaching to people who
knew nothing of and cared nothing for Christ,
that no one—or only one here and there—
bothered about the people in other lands.

But Carey's heart was tender as he thought of
their ignorance, and he longed to do something
about it. Every book about foreign parts that he
could lay hands on he read. He made a large map
and put it up on his schoolroom wall, and marked
up everything he discovered about the peoples
of the world, until it was a mine of information.

By the time William Carey was twenty-eight
he was talking and praying continually of taking
the Gospel to the heathen. Some people grew
impatient with him: surely there was enough work
to be done at home? But some sympathised,
particularly, Sutcliff, Ryland and Fuller.

Then Carey was invited to become the minister
of a Baptist church in Leicester, Harvey-lane.
This was a hard church to take over, for a great

many of the members lived worse lives than those who never darkened a church porch.

The congregation pretty well had to be taken to pieces and put together again before all was well. But by the time William had finished his reformation it was a chapel full of people who really loved the Lord.

But all the stress of putting things to rights: all the added duties a small salary made necessary—more shoe-making and school-teaching; continual study and the coming of a tiny daughter: even her loss after two sweet years, could not make Carey forget the heathen who knew nothing of the Lord Jesus Christ.

There came a day when a great number of ministers in Northamptonshire and Leicestershire held a united meeting, at which Sutcliff and Fuller preached. The sum total of what they had to say was that the churches in England *said* that they were praying for the conversion of the world, but they were *doing* nothing about it.

When the preaching was over Carey leaped to his feet, challenging the ministers to do something to start a missionary society there and then. But this was an unheard of thing! The ministers had liked the sermons, but they were still timid. Even Sutcliff and Fuller said they must wait a little longer.

Oh, that little longer! How it irked Carey's spirit. There at home he had a manuscript he had been writing, all about the world situation: some of its words seemed to come into his mind now . . .

It had come about like this: there was only one way in which an obscure pastor-shoemaker could make his views known to a large number of people in those days, and that was to write them down and have them published. So to his other work he had added the writing of a booklet in which he set out in orderly fashion, but with desperate earnestness, all the spiritual needs of the world, and the little that was being done by a few heroic missionaries. He worked out a sensible plan of how missionaries might live, helping to support themselves, and showed what the Christians of Britain could do, and how they could do it.

If the ministers disappointed him by their timidity—and they did—a few of them did at least muster enough courage to recommend him to get what he had written ready for publication, and publish it. That was better than nothing, and home went Carey to put the finishing touches to the manuscript which was to kindle missionary fire in many a heart.

By this time Carey was well known among the Nottinghamshire Baptists, so when the Ministers' Association had an important meeting in the spring of the year in which he was thirty-one, they asked him to be the speaker.

The sermon he preached that day fanned into flame the fire that had been so slow to kindle. Carey produced a sort of slogan, to challenge the bold and put courage into the faint-hearted:

Expect great things from God;
Attempt great things for God,

and there was a blaze of enthusiastic emotion from pastors and from people.

But by the time the ministers met alone for a meeting the next morning, some of their courage had evaporated. After all, they reasoned, they only represented a few small, poor churches. Who were to be the missionaries? How could they support them? Had they any right to undertake such a revolutionary action? The time was not yet ripe. Let them wait until they had some special sign from God. The task was beyond their strength. And so on . . . *And the members of the meeting began to get ready to go home.*

But Carey was on his feet. He gripped Fuller by the arm: "Is there nothing again going to be done, sir?" he asked desperately.

Passionately he pleaded with the ministers: now was the time, they *could not* put it off any longer . . .

Then Fuller rallied his adventurous courage, and stood by Carey; and the day was won. Carey might be a man with a bee in his bonnet; a wild youthful enthusiast. But when the Reverend Mr. Fuller of Kettering added his pleas the ministers threw off their fears and resolved that a plan should be prepared for the forming of "A Baptist Society for Propagating the Gospel among the Heathen." Which put into plain English meant a Baptist Missionary Society.

That was in May. In October the plan was ready—in Carey's mind and heart at least. That autumn the Baptist Association meetings were held in Fuller's chapel, at Kettering, on October 2nd: but the missionary question was not brought up at all at the public meetings.

In the evening, however, twelve of the ministers and two other Christians squeezed into the little back room of a home known as the "Gospel Inn": it was the house of a Mrs. Wallis, a widow who was known far and wide for her hospitality to preachers.

And there in that little back parlour—after some more doubting and hesitation, it must be confessed—the foundations of the Baptist Missionary Society were laid. The first subscription list was drawn up, with the pathetic total of £13 2s. 6d. made up of small sums of the widow's mite variety; and the wheels began to turn.

The Committee was appointed: Carey and his three friends, with Fuller as secretary, and the Rev. R. Hogg, as treasurer; and it was at the fourth meeting of that committee that Carey met the missionary challenge in a new way, in a way which was drastic in its effect upon his own every-day family life.

VI

GETTING UNDER WAY

IT's no good starting a missionary society unless
you have a missionary field. The trouble with
the Baptist Missionary Society was that they
hardly knew where to begin! Missionaries were so
few and far between that they had the whole
uncivilised world to choose from.

There were many confabulations in the Committee, and then one day Carey had a letter. It
was from a missionary doctor home from Bengal,
a Mr. John Thomas. John Thomas had meant
to be at the meeting when the plan was put
forward, but, just like John Thomas, he had
forgotten the time!

He was trying to raise funds to go back to
missionary work in Bengal, and he wanted to
find a companion, too, to go with him.

Naturally enquiries were made about him,
about the work he had done and the sort of man
he was; and finally the Committee asked him to
meet them for discussion.

On the appointed day, January 10th, 1793,
the Committee members all arrived at Kettering.
John Thomas did not arrive for a long time.
Being John Thomas he had hurt his foot, and it
was not until evening that he put in an appearance!

But during the day the Committee had had
plenty of time to talk the whole matter over, and

before evening they had made up their minds to accept the opportunity God had given them. They decided to invite Thomas to join the Society, and then turning to Carey, they said:

"Are you willing to go to India with Mr. Thomas?" Just like that.

But Carey was altogether willing and ready. It was not that it was an easy choice: he must leave his home, his country, his friends. But William Carey was not the man, when God said, "Go!" to answer, "Oh, but I *can't!*"

So by the time Thomas did arrive they welcomed him with open arms, and bombarded him with questions about himself, his life in India, and conditions there.

He had a lot to tell them: things had not always been easy for him in India, and he was pretty frank. John Thomas was one of those unfortunate people whose faults upset the greatest possible number of those they meet. We've all got our failings, but some of us manage to keep them to ourselves and our families. John Thomas did not.

One of his greatest drawbacks was that he had no sense at all about money. He was a hopeless business man, and did not know it. Mistaking rashness for faith, he was for ever plunging himself into debt. This was bad enough when he was alone, but when he and Carey joined forces it made a lot of trouble for William too.

But before we blame John Thomas too much, let us keep in mind that Carey never stopped loving him. And if the one who suffered most through him still loved him, we are not going to criticise. When his blunders crop up in the story they must be told, but we shall tell them, and think of them with no ill feeling.

That night Carey had to break the news at home, and a bitter task it proved. He had to tell his loving Dorothy that he was going to India. Then when she had got over the first shock of that, he asked her to go too.

But how could she? she demanded. With three little boys under eight, and another baby on the way, how could she leave her home and all those she loved, for a strange land and a strange people, speaking a strange language. No, she would not go. It was too much!

There was a strained, unhappy silence in the cottage that night as they settled down to sleep. Dorothy could hardly believe that her William would think of leaving her and the little ones. William could hardly believe that his Dorothy would refuse to go with him, when his going was just a simple matter of obeying God's call.

In the morning there were more tears and entreaties: but still Dorothy would not go: and William could not break his word. Fuller and Sutcliff came to the cottage to plead with her, but it was no use. She would not think of travelling *anywhere* with a baby coming. And how would her husband's health stand the climate of India, after his long fever, and that dreadful cough, not so many years ago? They knew he was not strong . . .

So it went on. But we are not going to blame

poor Dorothy any more than we blame William for being ready to leave her. His mind had been broadened by his reading: Dorothy did not even know how to read or write until after her marriage. He had for years been interested in the needs of the whole world: Dorothy's whole life and interest centred round Piddington, her home village, and the places nearby.

Other people, too, were grieved. William's congregation at Harvey-lane were full of sorrow that they were going to lose him: though they let him go readily, for the Lord's sake.

William's father could hardly believe his senses when he read the letter breaking the news. "Is William *mad?*" he exclaimed.

William was not mad, but he had taken on a difficult task. Obtaining money for passages, and for his and Thomas's support was a simple matter compared with the difficulties of gaining permission to enter India.

The great East India Company were in complete control, and *they did not like missionaries.* The law of the land would not allow anyone to visit India, let alone live there, without the Company's permission, so what was to be done? The worst of it was that no ship's captain would risk taking to India passengers who had not been given the Company's permission.

Carey and Thomas made one false start. Plans were all complete to sail on a ship, the *Earl of Oxford*; and Carey, his eight-year-old son Felix— whom Dorothy had agreed to allow to go with him—Mr. and Mrs. Thomas, and their little daughter were waiting in lodgings at Ryde, in the Isle of Wight, for the ship to sail.

Everything seemed perfectly in order, and Carey's mind was at last at rest about Dorothy. She and her sister Catherine, and the younger boys had settled down comfortably in a cottage he had found for them in her own village, and the new baby had safely arrived.

Naturally Carey was sore-hearted at parting with them, but he was at peace. "If I had all the world I would freely give it to have you and the dear children with me . . ." he wrote, in the loving letter he sent her a little while before they expected to sail.

But they did not sail. Someone wrote an anonymous letter to the captain of the ship, telling him that they were missionaries, and that he ran great risks if he carried them as his passengers. And the captain grew afraid, and refused to take any of them except Mrs. Thomas and the little girl. *He* wasn't going to be involved with the powerful East India Company.

Carey was almost heart-broken, and it was even harder for Thomas, who was already in trouble over his unhappy money affairs, and must now part with his wife and child, perhaps for months.

So the three, Carey, Thomas and little Felix, stood sadly on the jetty, watching the ship sail away. Back they went to London with heavy hearts. But after all it was for the best: as Carey wrote to Fuller, affairs were "superintended by an infinitely wise God."

Whether it was in sheer surprise at seeing her William again, when she had thought of him as sailing on the high seas, we cannot tell. But the joyous fact is that when Carey did go to see Dorothy at Piddington she agreed—after a good deal of pleading and argument—that she would go with him to India, taking the children, if her sister Catherine could go too. Catherine could go, and Catherine would go, so all was well.

It was John Thomas who came to hear of a Danish ship, the *Kron Princessa Maria*, which was going to India. The captain was willing to take them, all of them, and every difficulty was at last swept aside.

So early one June morning in 1793, Mr. and Mrs. Carey and all the little Careys, Catherine Plackett, and John Thomas came on board, and the great adventure had really begun.

VII

THE VOYAGE AND THE HARDSHIPS

THE blue waves danced to the far off horizon: the sea breeze blew sweet and keen, and as William Carey stood on deck it cooled his cheeks. It was so sweet, that he even removed his ugly, uncomfortable wig, that he might miss nothing of it.

Carey looked at the wig: such a clumsy thing, and if it looked horrible off, what must it look like on?

With a hasty glance round to make sure that there was no one to see, Carey flung the thing overboard into the blue water, and rejoiced to feel the wind ruffling the scanty, close-cropped hair which had begun to grow again, at least round the back of his head.

The voyage was pleasant now. Dorothy had got over her seasickness and her homesickness, and the children were thriving. Catherine was her usual helpful self. William had recovered from the fever which had troubled him not long after they sailed, and he and John Thomas were working away at the Bengali language. At other times he submerged himself in one or other of the seventy-seven parts of the *Botanical Magazine*, or the thirty-one parts of *English Botany!*

So the little missionary company were contented, and now William had got rid of his wig.

One problem, however, was always in their minds. What were they going to do when they reached India? Who would give them advice? What would they do if they were refused permission to land?

But when God sends people to a place, He sees that they stay there, if they are willing to obey Him. And the fact is that neither Carey nor his wife ever left India, once they got there, until they left it for heaven.

The *Kron Princessa Maria* sailed boldly up the estuary of the River Hooghli and when she reached Calcutta there was no one on board to whom the East India Company could raise the least objection. You see the objectionable people, the missionaries, had been quietly transferred at the estuary to a small native boat, which took them up-river.

How eagerly the little party scanned the banks of the new land, and how they stared at the villages they passed: and how the people stared at them! As they journeyed the tide turned against them, and the Indian boatman put in at a landing place near a small village until they could go on again, and with eager delight Carey sprang ashore. At last he was on Indian soil, in an Indian village. He did not know enough Bengali to preach to the people, much as he would have loved it; but Thomas did, and they listened to him for three solid hours.

To the delight of the children one of the Indians brought food for them, and they all sat on the

ground and ate rice and curry from plantain
leaves, using those fingers which were "made
before forks." It is to be hoped that the curry
did not prove too hot for the tender mouths
of the very young.

With the turn of the tide they were off again,
and the next day they landed quietly in Calcutta
and nobody even noticed them.

First of all Thomas had to find his wife and
daughter; then he had to find and rent a house
where the two families could live. He met someone else in Calcutta, too: a man he had led to the
Lord Jesus Christ during his last stay in India,
named Ram Ram Boshu. This man had not been
faithful to the Lord: but as he seemed truly sorry,
the missionaries agreed that he ought to be given
another chance, and he was taken on as Carey's
language teacher.

Thomas, unhappily, was entrusted with their
funds; and the way that man made the money dis-
appear had to be seen to be believed. Worst of all,
Carey now found that Thomas had left India in
debt, and his creditors were on his track. And very
soon the money they had set out with was all gone.

There was a good deal of travelling about in
search of work for Carey, but in the end they had
to agree to separate: Thomas to set up in Calcutta
as a doctor, and Carey to find some means of
keeping himself and his family.

There they were, stranded in a strange city,
in a foreign land, destitute. Dorothy was worn
out with the unsettled life, and she was frankly

nervy and cross. Catherine too was complaining and the children none too well. The curry and rice did not suit any of them, and they longed for an honest loaf instead of the stodgy, round, flat Indian *chapatis*. Then Dorothy and the two older boys fell sick with dysentery, and Felix was soon very dangerously ill.

But the Lord was taking care of them all, and the day came when they were ready to fulfil Carey's dream of going up into the country, building a simple hut, and living like the natives, that they might win the natives for Christ. Carey had been offered a piece of land at a place called Deharta, some three days' journey up-river from Calcutta: and after many difficulties Thomas managed to obtain enough money to make it possible for them to set off.

So one Monday morning in February a boat was loaded up with their baggage and the few pieces of furniture Carey possessed: Catherine stepped gingerly in: Dorothy and Felix, still ill, were helped in: the baby and little William were handed in: the menfolk got in, and the Indian oarsmen began to row.

That was a journey of thrills and terrors, and of real hardship. It was hot, and their way lay through narrow, salty waterways and across a wide, salt lake.

Yet there was a world of loveliness in the rich, tropical plants and trees, and especially in the palm trees which fringed the river; and it all delighted Carey's nature-loving soul.

As they passed one village Carey gave a shout:
"*Stop!*" For there under a rough shed stood a
huge idol, hung with garlands of flowers: strangely
clad priests and a number of "musicians" made
various unpleasant noises with flutes and tom-
toms. And all the while villagers came with their
offerings, baskets of brilliantly coloured fruit
and bowls of rice, to gain the favour of the hideous,
man-made thing they worshipped. How Carey
longed to speak to them as they halted, watching:
but for the time being, as far as they were concerned he was as good as dumb.

Then they came to a terrifying region, the
tiger-haunted swamps called the Sunderbunds.
Here rivers and creeks crossed and re-crossed
hundreds of square miles of thick jungle, almost
uninhabited by man, but very much inhabited
by tigers, leopards, rhinoceroses, buffaloes, mon-
keys which chattered in the trees, and pythons
and cobras which made their stealthy way through
the undergrowth: and on the mudbanks by the
river the crocodiles lay, malignant, basking in
the hot sunshine.

Dorothy and Catherine were openly terrified,
and the children reflected their panic. When the
little boat was obliged to tie up on the bank, no
one, not even Ram Ram Boshu or the Indian
boatmen, dared to go more than a hundred yards
away from the boat. Their nights were disturbed
by the jungle noises, by the croaking frogs, the
chorus of crickets, and by the humming of
swarming mosquitoes—who soon added to the

little party's discomforts by their irritating attentions.

But the heavenly Father had them in His care: and not the least of His miracles was that William Carey, who had had to leave landwork because he was so sensitive to sunlight, had not a trace of his old skin trouble then, or ever after.

At last the journey ended, and the boat drew in to the little landing stage near the flat-roofed bungalow with a semi-circular verandah, which was to be their home if it was not already occupied. *But it was occupied.* The screened windows were opened to the morning air: and a few Indians idling round the place made it all too plain that someone else was in possession of the home they had hoped for.

For a while there was consternation in the little boat. There were feeble reproaches from Dorothy, and vigorous protests from Catherine, while the children listened to their elders with wide-opened eyes and trembling lips. What were they to do *now*? Catherine demanded. Dorothy felt too ill for anything but a sullen silence after her first querulous outburst. They could hardly camp out in this tiger-infested region, Catherine went on, and on . . .

But it was all right. All the fuss was for nothing. It would have been better to trust God first, and ask questions afterwards.

Living in the bungalow at that time was Mr. Charles Short, and he was out shooting with his dog that morning. Great was his surprise when he saw the pitiful little company of sick and weary Europeans stumbling out of the boat.

He hurried down to them, and with eager hospitality he welcomed them into his home. And oh, the bliss of a real home again, after that awful journey. It was so delightful to be waited on and cared for. In a matter of hours the invalids were beginning to improve, and Catherine was happily settled with the little ones: and Carey and Mr. Short began to talk.

Mr. Short did not think much of their missionary hopes: "Absurd!" he exclaimed. "The Indian people would never listen: and if they would, they're not worth going after!" And he did not disguise the fact that he had a pretty poor opinion of religion in general, anyway.

But that did not prevent him from proving the kindest of friends. Carey told him of his plan to build a house, and of his disappointed hopes that they might have found the bungalow empty.

"Well, it's *not* empty," Mr. Short said roundly. "But you're just going to stay here with me— the whole lot of you—until you've got somewhere ready. Stay half a year if you like. I shall be only too pleased to have you, and there's plenty of room!"

But they did not stay there for long, after all, for soon exciting news came from Thomas in Calcutta. He had met an old friend, Mr. Udney, a Christian who owned two indigo factories: and he had asked Thomas to go as overseer to one of them. Thomas promptly accepted, and as promptly suggested Carey as a good man to manage the other one.

Carey was in no doubt. The family were fit as they had not been for months, and to the delight of them all, Catherine and Mr. Short had fallen in love and were to be married.

It meant yet another apprenticeship it was true, for he knew nothing about the manufacture of indigo. But it would provide him with an assured salary, and leave him plenty of time for language study: and under his care would be numerous workmen, all needing a Saviour, of whom Carey could tell them.

VIII

SERAMPORE

MR. William Carey, thirty-five year old indigo
planter (and missionary) of Mudnabatty, sat at
his desk. Out in the fields his employees were
busy in the blazing sunlight: in the great vats
more workmen were busy extracting the dye from
the plants: in the factory itself great furnaces
heated the boilers in which the dye was prepared
for packaging; and. in the packing department
there was a steady hammering as the crates were
closed up . . . And it was all directed by Mr.
Carey, indigo planter (and missionary).

At home in England Carey had lived and
thought in terms of shillings and pence, and he
was pastor to a little handful of people. Here he
was handling large sums of money, and was
controlling hundreds of men. The humble,
obscure life he had dreamed of among the village
people, living as they did, was not for him. Later
on, under Carey's leadership, others were to
open up many such little mission posts. But Carey
was capable of the greater responsibilities, and
so, of course, God made him ready for them.

Many things had happened since he had settled
down at Mudnabatty, six years ago. He had
learned to deal with the Indians: he had learned
just how hard he could drive himself in that
climate—and specially in the monsoon weather—

and just how hard he could *not* drive himself.

He had learned first-hand of the horrors of heathenism and idolatry; and in talking with his workpeople he came to understand the Indian outlook upon life. He had learned once more to make acquaintance with sorrow, for at a time when he himself had been desperately ill with fever, his little five-year old son Peter had died. He had learned to bear an even more bitter grief, the fact that poor Dorothy began to develop mental trouble, so that she could give him neither care nor companionship.

He had learned not only to speak, and preach, and write in Bengali, he had learned to *think* in Bengali: and by the time he had been at Mudnabatty a few months he had produced a Bengali grammar and vocabulary, and translations of Genesis, Matthew, Mark, and the epistle of James.

Naturally as soon as the translations were ready, Carey was eager to get them printed. But how could this be done? There was, as yet, no Bengali type in existence, and if he had the necessary punches sent out from England, and made it himself, it would cost thousands of pounds to print only ten thousand copies of the New Testament.

He had learned just how wonderfully God meets every need as it arises. Just at that time they began to make the type he needed in Calcutta. And what was more, he heard of a printing press which was for sale for £46 only. Best of all, kind Mr. Udney bought the press himself, and had it sent up to Mudnabatty as a gift.

The press arrived on a Sunday, and it was an awful temptation to Carey, who longed to go straight down and fetch it at once. But he would not do that: the family thanked God and waited till Monday. The amusing thing was that when this queer, squat machine was set up, the Indians called it "the sahib's idol"! They did not know that its purpose was the destruction of the *Indian* idols.

He had learned a vast amount about the natural history of India: there had been time for his boyhood hobby, and he kept the closest, most detailed records of the flowers, trees, animals, fish, birds and insects, discovering all their native names, and asking a thousand questions of the curious Indians—who probably thought him a very strange being to bother about such trivial matters.

Every Sunday when the factory was closed, and two or three evenings in the week, Carey used to go out to the villages preaching. There were no roads, so he would tramp along the ridged, narrow paths between the rice fields, often covering twenty miles a day: and he learned a host of things in this way about the people's daily lives.

But above all he had learned the lesson of his own memorable sermon, that those who attempt great things for God may expect great things from God.

On this particular day as Carey sat at his desk he was busy studying another of the languages of India, Sanskrit, his Indian teacher standing at his side.

Suddenly they were interrupted. "A visitor for you, sir! A sahib!" the Indian servant announced.

And there on the verandah stood an Englishman, and what was more, he was a missionary; and what was more still, he was a missionary of the Baptist Missionary Society.

Carey could hardly believe his eyes and ears. True, in a few of the recent letters from home there had been vague hints of the possibility of sending him help one of these days, but he had had no word of this young man's coming.

John Fountain his name was. He had managed to travel in one of the East India Company's own ships, by going steerage—a procedure little short of heroic at that time—as somebody's servant. Somehow he had managed to land in Calcutta without any questions being asked. Somehow here he was, in Carey's study.

Fountain was soon introduced to Indian life, and he had many surprises. As he quaintly put it: "I had thought to sit in farmers' chimney corners, as in Rutland (where he came from), and get a basin of milk. But I found farmers not distinguishable from other folks: and there are no chimneys in Bengal. I was rarely asked in to any houses, and when I was, there seemed to be nothing within them!"

John Fountain did Carey good. He had been

so lonely, the only white man for miles, and his Dorothy was too ill in her mind to give him any friendship. It was grand to have Christian companionship. And before long Fountain had persuaded Carey to come with him for a daily swim in the river, and every morning they would race across to the white sands on the other side.

Perhaps Carey's life was becoming a little bit too serious. Perhaps in those days he was in danger of forgetting that he was not only the William Carey who had always been fascinated by study, but also the boy who had had a name for courage and fun.

So Fountain used to drag him away from his work at times, for a little relaxation. Probably the Indians thought them both crazy: it was all very well for little boys to play in the water, and no one objected to religious immersion in the sacred Ganges: but this . . . Still, it did Carey all the good in the world: God does not ask that any man in His service shall turn into a complete sobersides.

Fountain's arrival made Carey all the more eager for other reinforcements: he redoubled his appeals to the Committee in England. And truly they and the friends of the Mission were doing their utmost. More and more people in Britain were growing interested in missionary work: more and more money was being collected, and gradually men and women began to volunteer to serve abroad.

Carey told the Committee that a missionary

party could gain admission to India by signing on as his assistants in the indigo factory: and as he was convinced that all missionaries ought to take on some sort of work that they might help to support themselves, the idea was sound.

Nine months after that letter reached England four missionaries were on their way to India.

There was William Ward, a printer from Derby. Before Carey had left England he had met this man, and challenged him: "We shall want *you* in India in a few years, to print the Bible: you must come after us!" And Ward had never forgotten that moment.

There was a school teacher with his wife— Joshua and Hannah Marshman—and their two children, who packed up their belongings and left home for India at three weeks' notice.

There were Mr. and Mrs. Grant and their two children, Mr. and Mrs. Brunsden, and Miss Tidd, who was going out to marry Fountain.

Before their ship reached Calcutta the authorities had found out that they were a missionary party, so they all made their way to the Danish settlement of Serampore, where the East India Company had no authority.

The Danish governor, Colonel Bie, was most kind and helpful. He could do nothing to help them to settle *out* of Serampore, he said, but he could and would welcome the whole mission to stay there, and work from there. Why, he asked, did not Carey come and join them, instead of their trying to go to Carey?

So they settled down where they could, to wait as well as they could, until they knew what Carey decided. Then there came a heavy blow: Mr. Grant took fever, and even before they had realised that he was in any danger, he was dead. That was a sad loss for the Mission: but at least the general situation looked happier. Colonel Bie assured them that they could carry on their work without hindrance. They could open schools, which would not only bring the Gospel to the children, but would earn money to support the missionaries. They could set up their printing press there, and print all the Scriptures and tracts they wished; and they were free to distribute as many as they were able.

Carey said, Yes. Of course, it meant a considerable loss of money to him personally, but he wasn't the man to worry about that, in the light of the welfare of the Mission.

Soon the printing press and the precious type he had accumulated were safely packed up and sent off with the Careys' other belongings. They said goodbye to all their Indian friends and then Carey and his three boys, and poor Dorothy—who was by now hopelessly ill mentally, though able to travel—set off for Serampore.

And on January 10th, 1800 he reached the place where his greatest work was to be done, and, sad to say, his greatest sorrows and difficulties to be borne.

No bamboo and grass huts for the Mission in Serampore. There on the river bank, with a good plot of land around it, was a fine house, with one specially large room which would make a splendid chapel. It was for sale, and although it cost a good deal of money, people who *trust* always find that God sends the money for things needed for His work.

Soon all was settled, and the missionaries moved in. Each family had its own rooms, but they had their meals all together: good Mrs. Marshman looked after the Carey family, as well as her own.

It was agreed that whatever they did to earn money, all should go into the common fund: and that each family should take charge of the housekeeping for a month, turn and turn about. Carey was general treasurer, and had charge of the medicine chest—for Thomas kept on indigo planting, visiting them frequently—and all their books were put into a common library, with Fountain as librarian.

We don't know whether Saturday night was bath night, but it *was* the night when they cleaned up their friendships! If there had been any trouble or quarrelling in the week—and even missionaries can fall out with one another at times—on Saturday night the trouble was talked over and settled, so that each Sunday began a new week with sweet and kindly feelings. It was a first class plan for the preservation of a happy family.

Since it was never too soon to begin a Baptist church in Serampore, they formed themselves into one, with Carey as pastor and Fountain and Marshman as deacons.

It was not long before they were all busy. Ward with Brunsden's help set up the printing press in a building at the side of the house: the type was unpacked and set out ready for use: the supply of paper received from England was most carefully stored—for they wanted it to *print on,* not for the nourishment of innumerable hoards of creatures! Then Ward began to set up the type to print with. It was slow work printing, at first. They had only enough type for one page, and in any case the press was old fashioned, and would only print one sheet at a time.

But within three months Ward came joyously to Carey one day, with the first sheet of the Bengali New Testament.

Felix was a great help to him by now. He was fifteen, and because he had spoken Bengali since he was a little boy, he was invaluable. Thirteen-year-old William, too, was beginning to make himself useful.

Soon Ward had another helper. Ram Ram Boshu, Carey's old language teacher, who had left them for a time, came back to Carey. He was an excellent Bengali scholar and a good writer, and so they set him to writing tracts, which Ward printed off in large numbers.

Carey and Fountain were busy preaching all the time, and when the tracts were ready, they found them most useful. Gradually the Indians grew used to the missionaries, and learned to trust them, and *they began to think*. But it was a long time before they could write home of any converts: and before that joyous day did come, Fountain had died of fever.

The Marshmans were fully occupied, too. By the time Ward had produced his first page of the New Testament they had opened two boarding schools for Europeans, one for boys and one for girls. A month later they opened a school for Indians, and before long there were forty boys there, all eager to learn English, and English ways, and English subjects.

In less than a year Marshman knew enough Bengali to do a little preaching; and though Ward was not such a quick learner, he used to take Felix out with him, and sometimes the boy even preached himself.

The printing of the Word of God was rightly considered one of their most important tasks. Soon the press was employing a compositor, a folder, and a binder, in addition to Ward, Brunsden and Felix. They were printing six thousand half-sheets a week, working as hard as they could go.

But printing was a costly business, and the money began to run out. Nothing daunted, they put an advertisement in a Calcutta newspaper: they were wishing to print Scriptures, and they suggested that people who would like a copy should pay for it in advance. People did like, and from then on their money problem was solved, as far as printing-bills were concerned.

But that advertisement gave rise to other trouble: trouble which turned out to be very useful! The Governor General of India, Lord Wellesley, was not at all pleased to learn that these missionaries were printing anything at all: he was quite determined to bring it to a stop.

But before he took active steps he had the sense to consult his chaplain, the Rev. David Brown. Mr. Brown knew Carey well by now, and he spoke so highly of him and his friends, and so movingly about the great good that the Word of God could do in Indian hearts and minds, that soon the prejudice was all gone.

IX

CONVERSIONS AND EXPANSION

THERE was great jubilation in the Serampore family. They had made their first convert at last!

In Serampore there lived a poor carpenter, a Hindu—and Hindus were very hard to bring to Christ. Krishna Pal was his name. Now one day Krishna Pal slipped, and dislocated his shoulder, and as Thomas was with the missionary family at the time, he went at once with Carey and Marshman to see what could be done to help the poor man.

Of course in those days there was no X-ray: though in any case this injury was all too easy to diagnose. And there was no chloroform. Poor Krishna Pal was tied firmly to a tree: Carey and Marshman held out his arm, and Thomas jerked the bone back into its socket.

"I am a great sinner! A great sinner am I! Save me, sahib, save me!" yelled the poor sufferer, hardly knowing what he was saying in his agony.

But Thomas took what he said seriously, and showed himself a good psychologist. He knew that a man in Krishna Pal's condition at that moment could not listen to long and convincing arguments! As he bound the injured shoulder he simply repeated the same text over and over again, ten times, putting it into an Indian poetic form, to help Krishna Pal to remember it: "He that covereth his sins shall not prosper; but whoso confesseth and forsaketh them shall find mercy."

The Hindu went off home for a few days in bed, with a comforted shoulder, and some good words in his mind.

One day, when he was up and about again, he met Thomas in the street.

"Sahib!" he said, "I am a very great sinner, but I have confessed my sin . . . and *I am free!*" This was the first conversion in the history of the Baptist Missionary Society.

Every day after that Krishna Pal came to the Mission for teaching, and soon his wife and daughter and his best friend Goluk, had made up their minds that they, too, would walk the Jesus way.

The day of Krishna Pal's baptism was probably the most exciting day Carey had known since he set foot in India. At last their first convert was publicly confessing the Lord Jesus Christ as his Saviour, and he was a caste man.

Krishna Pal and Carey's first son Felix were both baptised, European and Indian confessing the same Lord the same day. Goluk and the women had taken fright at the last moment, but their turn came later on.

There was only one cloud: the excitement and the joy of this event had so upset poor Thomas that he too, like Dorothy, grew mentally ill. And from that time there was little he could do to help the Serampore Mission, even after he had recovered. But he did not live long. God wanted him in heaven, where his hopeless business irresponsibility was forgotten, and the only fact in his life which was remembered was his undying love for the Lord who had saved him, and his unfailing eagerness to bring others to Him.

At about the same time that Thomas died, Brunsden, too, fell incurably ill; and his death meant that out of the seven missionaries sent out by the Baptist Missionary Society, only three were left. But what a three they were!

Soon they came to be known as the "Serampore Triad," and from this time onward we shall find that Carey's life can hardly be thought of apart from the lives of his two friends.

The work was growing on every hand. After three years there were thirteen baptised Bengalis. The schools developed so fast that in October 1801 they had to buy a large house and grounds next door to the one they owned: and within two years the schools alone were making an income of nearly a thousand pounds a year for the Mission.

In that same year the Bengali New Testament was completed—most of it set up by Ward, with Felix's help. That was a joyous day when the first bound copy was taken into the little chapel and laid on the Communion table, and all the mission family and the baptised converts met together for glad thanksgiving.

The missionaries by now were going out in pairs farther afield, among the villages, taking

Scriptures and tracts, and preaching wherever they could. Sometimes they would take converts with them: and Krishna Pal went with Ward on his very first tour.

But William Carey was not only set upon doing positive good: he was set against positive evil. And there were terrible evils in India. There was, for one thing, nothing less than open baby-murder. Every January at the full moon there was a great Hindu festival, held where the river Ganges empties into the sea. One of the ways in which devoted Hindu mothers showed their religious devotion, was to throw their babies into the sacred river, where they drowned, or experienced the tender mercies of crocodiles or sharks.

The British government did not wish to "upset the native religious customs," so they did nothing. But Mr. Udney, the indigo planter, was a good Christian man, and at last he was able to bring the matter before Lord Wellesley. When Wellesley agreed to a formal enquiry, Udney suggested William Carey as the best man for the job, and the Governor General agreed.

Carey was more than willing. Never had he forgotten a little dead baby he and Thomas had found cast out from its home because the family thought it was bewitched, as it was sick, and feeble.

Carey's report to the government was a fiery report, and an effective one. A new law was made, and the very next year at the festival Indian soldiers were stationed along the banks of the river to see that the new law was obeyed. And from that time onward baby-sacrifice became a thing of the past.

Another evil was not so easily stamped out. Hindus burn the bodies of their dead—not a bad practice in a very hot climate, some people think. But there was another terrible custom. The widow of a dead man was allowed, more she was expected, to submit to being burned alive on her husband's funeral pyre: *sati* the Indians called it.

Carey never forgot the one time that he saw a *sati*. The only thing which kept him on the spot was his agonised hope that he could put a stop to it. With all his power, all his words, he tried to persuade that poor, misguided woman to give up her determination: to induce the heartless on-lookers to intervene. But that time he failed. Still, it nerved him as nothing else could to set himself against the evil.

Soon he was chosen to make an official investigation of *that* subject. He employed a number of reliable Indians and sent them to discover and report on all the burnings in a certain area round Calcutta. They heard of four hundred, and working on that figure they reckoned that in the provinces of Bengal ten thousand people went to this death every year.

This report of Carey's also went to the authorities: and although it was twenty-five years before something was done, the atrocity was at last stamped out.

It was a Sunday morning, and he sat in his study busy on his sermon, when a courier from the Governor General arrived with an urgent dispatch, which Carey was asked to translate into Bengali immediately.

Carey frowned. Was the Lord's Day the day for translating government documents? But one glance at the paper swept the frown away. He leaped to his feet, threw off his best Sunday coat, and set to work.

The document was an edict abolishing *sati* throughout British Dominions in India! Someone was sent to find one of the others to take the Sunday service: and I dare say that few other documents have been translated so quickly.

"If I delay a moment to translate and publish this edict," Carey thought, "Who knows how many widows' lives may be lost?" And the edict was published and put into effect in double quick time.

X

TRIALS AND TRIBULATIONS

THE missionaries never forgot their agreement to pay everything they earned into the common pool. Even when the Marshmans were making such a lot of money from their schools they lived in the simplest manner, just like the others, and paid all the money that was left into the Mission.

Soon Carey, too, was earning a high salary; but he did just the same. Lord Wellesley opened a college for Europeans in Calcutta, and plain William Carey was appointed Professor William Carey, teacher of Bengali! He used to go in to Calcutta on Tuesday evenings, and return to Serampore for the weekends. It was hard work at first, for Carey was nervous: he was not at all certain that he could cope with lively students! But he could: they all loved him, and before his first term was ended he was asked to teach Sanskrit as well.

One great handicap in the beginning was that there were literally no Bengali or Sanskrit books suitable for use: they just did not exist. But Carey was not to be beaten: he just turned to and produced them himself. He called in his old friend and teacher, Ram Ram Boshu, and together they compiled a Sanskrit and a Bengali grammar, and many other text books.

Another advantage of Carey's new work was that it put him in touch with many celebrated Indian teachers, or *pundits*, as they called them, who helped him enormously in the revisions of his translations.

More and more the Serampore missionaries were eager to see the *whole* Bible translated, not only into Bengali, but into Sanskrit and Hindi and Marathi, and all the many other languages of India.

It would mean for all of them hard, hard work: for though unconverted *pundits* could supply them with mere words, and prevent mistakes in language, only men who knew and had experienced the life that is in the Word of God could produce a true translation.

Marshman worked harder than ever at his own language study, and so did Ward. Ward had another task, too, that of preparing type, for many of these languages had never yet been put into print.

By now there were several more missionaries to help with the station work and other tasks: one came out in 1803, four more in 1805, and Felix himself was formally accepted as a missionary by the Society at home.

So the translation work went on furiously, until one of Carey's *pundits* exclaimed in astonishment to Ward: "What kind of body has Carey sahib? He never seems hungry nor tired, and never leaves a thing till it's finished!"

There were great troubles, as well as wonderful

advances. Lord Wellesley was recalled to England, and the man who came in his place did all he could to change his policy. All the old antagonism of the East India Company seemed to revive.

Travelling was hindered by demands for passports: government permission to build a mission station at Jessore was refused. Two new missionaries, Mr. Robinson and Mr. Chater, who came out during this time were forbidden to leave Calcutta without permission: and when Carey protested he was flatly told by the authorities that from then on the missionaries must not preach to the natives any more, nor allow their Indian converts to do so. They must not distribute pamphlets nor let others do so: they must not send out Indian evangelists *nor take any steps to persuade the Indian peoples to become Christians.*

This was terrible, and for a time they fought what seemed a losing battle. But at last the Rev. David Brown went to the Governor General in person, and succeeded in gaining some concessions. Even so the work was terribly hindered, and it was only after considerable trouble that Robinson and Chater were smuggled in to Serampore.

Then anti-missionary feeling was stirred up in England: questions were asked in parliament and a veritable campaign was conducted against Serampore, by people who affirmed that Christianity was stirring up trouble in India!

But the bad days passed, and the time came when once again there was liberty for the missionaries in India; and the uproar in Britain, painful as it had been, probably made the country as much missionary-conscious as anything could have done.

Through it all the Bible translation and the printing had gone on. Finally type was ready for ten oriental languages, and Carey wrote home saying that if they had the money at Serampore, in fifteen years they could have the Bible translated and printed in all the languages of the East.

Soon Andrew Fuller was busy at home raising the money which was needed.

Even Carey's daily life was multi-lingual. Here is just one day's programme: At a quarter to six he got up and read a chapter from the *Hebrew* Bible, and had his "quiet time." At seven he conducted family prayers in *Bengali*. While he waited for his breakfast he spent some time reading *Persian* with a teacher, and then a portion of Scripture in *Hindustani*. That's four languages before breakfast!

After breakfast he settled down to *Sanskrit* translation. From ten till two he was at the college, teaching *English* youths: then he read *Bengali* proofs until dinner time, after which he translated some of the Gospel of Matthew into *Sanskrit* with a *pundit* until six, when he studied *Telugu*. At half past seven he preached in *English*, and finished the day by reading in the New Testament in *Greek*.

It was at this point, when every branch of the work was in full swing, that there came tragedy.

XI

THE FIRE

THE day's work was over in the Mission printing works. The crashing and the thumping of the printing presses had stopped: the clatter of wooden galley trays, of leaden type, the cheerful chatter of dozens of soft-and-high-voiced Indian workmen were silenced.

Two or three workmen were still there, finishing off odd jobs. Ward was still there, making up the day's accounts in his little office. Marshman had gone home, a little more slowly than usual, and sadly, because only a week before his baby son had died. So he sat at home, quietly, rather melancholy. Carey, of course, was in the college in Calcutta, for it was the middle of the week.

The brilliant sunshine began to fade, and Ward began to think of putting his account books away. No good straining his sight . . . Then he awoke to the fact that he was straining another sense: he sat up, tense and perfectly still, and he *sniffed*. He sniffed again. Smoke! Then in a second he was on his feet and out of the room. For if there is one dread in a printing works, it is the dread of fire. Stacked paper can smoulder unnoticed for a fearfully long time, so that all too often a fire has gained a desperate hold before it is discovered.

Ward lost no time. At full speed he ran down the

length of the long, low composing-room, with its wooden benches and type-racks, and its litter of paper. At the other end was the paper store-room, and, ominously, from around the door frame there came lazy, wispy trails of acrid smoke.

Ward opened his mouth and shouted at the top of his voice:

"Fire! Fire!"

The Indian servants heard him: they came running, shouting as they ran, their soft voices shrill with excitement and fear:

"Fire! Fire!"

Marshman in his nearby house, was awakened out of his sad musing, and came running over: he too shouted:

"*Fire! Fire!*"

Ward reached the store room first, the two Indians hard on his heels. He flung open the door, and then he blenched in sheer horror.

Stacked on great stages were reams and reams of paper—twelve hundred reams in all. And it was one of those stages which was smouldering, giving off great clouds of that stinging, particularly unpleasant smoke which comes from burning paper.

As Ward hesitated for very shock, the two Indians ran in past him, down toward the burning shelf. But by now the room was thick with smoke, and they were driven back to the door, where one of them promptly collapsed: excitement, fear, half-suffocation had been too much for him. By now Marshman was on the scene, and he and the other Indian picked up the fainting man and carried him where the air was clearer. He soon revived, and by the time Ward had decided what must be done, he was able to help again.

By now there were other helpers at hand. People appeared from everywhere, Europeans and Indians, servants and neighbours, all eager to help—and it must be confessed, all eager to see what was going on.

Ward gave his orders promptly and calmly, now that he had recovered from his first shock.

"First, every window and door shut!" he commanded. And it was done in a moment.

"Now, *please*," Ward appealed to the crowd, "will you bring from your houses all the pots and water jars you can find, and fill them up from the river as quickly as you can?"

Half the crowd promptly dispersed: some were still busy at the doors and windows, and some were just those helpless, hopeless people who can only stand and watch when somebody else's tragedy is in the making.

Meanwhile Ward and Marshman, with a few reliable helpers, had climbed the inevitable oriental outside staircase, and made their way on to the flat roof immediately over the paper store room.

Hastily, with such tools as they could muster, they began to break a hole in the roof. It was hard work, and uneasy work, with the thought of that smoky inferno under their very feet. Before they had quite broken through, Ward went over to the edge of the roof, and shouted down to the people, who by now were standing with their jars and pots, brass bowls and jugs and other vessels, dripping in their hands, water slopping on to the ground.

"Make a chain, please," Ward shouted, "and pass the water pots from hand to hand. And some of you folk without pots and pans, will you make another line, and pass back the empty ones to the river for refilling?"

Ward was a good organiser. Before long the supply of water was coming in a steady stream, and was poured through the hole right on to the site of the fire. But it was such a pathetic little stream: fast though they worked, it seemed so hopelessly inadequate.

Yet it began to have its effect, and for four solid hours, long after darkness had fallen, they slaved on and on valiantly. At last Ward straightened up.

"You know, I believe we're doing it!" he exclaimed to weary Marshman, passing a grimy hand over his dripping forehead. And they were. And it was at that very moment, through someone's excited folly, that all the good they had achieved was undone. No one knew quite who was to blame: probably someone just couldn't resist the temptation to open a window and have a look at the damage, now that the fire was in hand.

From his place on the roof Ward stiffened: down there in the smoky room he suddenly saw a new red glow beginning. Rapidly it spread, and once more he felt the hot draught fanning his face. All too soon he understood what had happened. Desperately he ran to the edge of the roof and shouted:

"Someone's opened a window! For mercy's sake shut it, or it'll all be ablaze again. Quickly! *Quickly!*"

But the damage was done. It was as though a damper had been opened in a great furnace. In rushed the air through the opened window, and in less time than it takes to tell, that red heart of fire had burst into flames, and soon great tongues of fire were pouring through the hole in the roof, which now served as a great chimney.

"Down!" Ward ordered, in the flat tones of hopelessness. "That has finished it!"

Hastily Marshman and the others scrambled down the stairs, and Ward followed, despair in his heart.

"Save the presses! Save the presses!" Ward gasped next. And breathlessly, utterly weary though they were, he and Marshman and the others rushed round to the little annexe built on to the side of the main works. Somehow they did it. Somehow those five cumbersome great machines were moved to safety—though just then it was hard to stop to be thankful in the midst of so much bitter, hopeless loss.

"The dormitories'll be next, if we don't take care!" Marshman suddenly said. And soon a crowd of excited, frightened children were marched out into a neighbour's house, while the bedding and furniture from their building was taken out to safety. There was nothing else to be done. Fortunately this was a false alarm: and certainly the children had no complaints to make about such an exciting break in routine.

Ward and Marshman's helpers suddenly seemed to lose their heads altogether. While the pair of them were busy salvaging all that was precious from the little office—documents, account books, records, manuscripts—other people had opened the composing room windows, to see if they could save anything there, making fresh and yet more furious draughts. The place had been filled with smoke: soon it was filled with flames. The wooden benches caught fire in a few moments, helped by the paper that was lying about. Nothing could be moved, and with the help of new currents of air the whole place was soon blazing furiously.

In silence now the great crowd of people stood in the reddened darkness, watching the raging inferno which had been such a hive of industry. They watched until midnight, and then, with a crashing and rending the roof fell in.

A gasp went up from the people as a huge tongue of flame and a fountain of sparks shot right up into the sky. Let *that* swerve to one side or the other, some thought, and who can tell what trouble may come from it?

But by the mercy of God it "burned straight as a candle flame," as Marshman put it; and even the showering sparks and burning fragments did no more damage.

Two hours later the fire had burnt itself out. Wearily, miserably, with reddened eyes, aching throats and blackened hands and faces, reeking with smoke, Ward and Marshman and their helpers made their way to their homes. Soon the crowd had dispersed too, and the few remaining hours of darkness mercifully hid the desolation.

Morning brought full realisation of what had been lost. In the composing-room last evening the work had lain just as the men had left it. "Copy," type, galleys, proofs, all were gone. Fifty-five thousand printed sheets had been at one end of the room ready for folding: there were precious manuscripts of Scripture translations, grammars, books, tracts . . . all were gone.

All that remained of the building was a black-ened shell, and Ward and Marshman stood hope-lessly looking at it.

"I must go and break the news to Carey, Ward," Marshman said despairingly.

"Yes," said Ward. "*Yes!*"

Marshman set off for Calcutta at once, and Ward began a heartbreaking search among the blackened ruins. He found half-burned books, and the sad remains of dirty, soaked papers. He found metal for making type melted into great flakes, lying on the earth floor—three and a half tons of it.

Hours of work cleared the place where the machine-room had been: and there, weary and wretched as he was, Ward gave a great shout of joy. The precious punches used to make type, and the matrices of all the Indian type—which had taken ten years to make—were practically unharmed.

Meanwhile Marshman went to his bitter task. Never had the boat journey to Calcutta passed so swiftly: the moment he so dearly longed to put off seemed to rush upon him. All too soon he was there. How was he to tell Carey?

Then he was facing Carey, and Carey needed to give him one look only, to know that he was bringing terrible news.

"What is it?"

Out poured the unhappy story. In absolute silence Carey listened, quite overwhelmed. But Carey was a man, and he was God's man. Valiantly he rallied his courage. Valiantly he took his classes that day, and then with Marshman caught the afternoon tide to Serampore. They talked long in the boat, and drew very near to one another, those two friends in their distress.

Before they had arrived at Serampore Carey was full of plans for getting the press going again. The irreplaceable manuscripts of his which had been lost, were going to be replaced: and they were going to be better than they had ever been before.

Not a moment was lost. Only the previous Saturday a warehouse which they had let, had—to their dismay at the time—been left empty. Carey had only been back a day when the master moulder was installed there, already making fresh type from the flaky lumps of melted metal.

That same morning they gathered together the fifty or sixty workpeople, who stood anxious and unhappy, waiting for dismissal. But no dismissal came. Instead the *pundits* and type casters were set to work at once, and gladly worked in relays, day and night. The compositors, printers and binders were given their full wages and a month's leave: by which time they were to come back, ready to work, work, work.

That was March. By the end of July they were printing again in seven languages: two others were nearly ready. By the end of the year they had as much oriental type as they had ever had, and by the following April they were printing in more languages than before the fire.

The loss in terms of pounds, shillings and pence had been terrible, more than nine thousand pounds: but in two short months Christians in Britain had sent in so much money that Fuller had to tell the Committee to stop people from sending more.

It takes more than a conflagration to hinder God's work when men of God are willing to spend themselves undaunted.

XII

HAPPY ENDING

STILL the work went on growing: more men
came from England; more stations were established, and schools were opened at the stations,
where the Indian boys and girls could be educated. A splendid college was built—which
is still standing today—for the education of
Indian youths who were considered fit for the
ministry.

And still troubles came: Carey's garden, by
this time a botanical garden famous all over
civilised India—was flooded by the river. At
another time a cyclone blew down many of his
rare and lovely trees, one of them right on top of
his greenhouses.

But this sort of trouble Carey could cope with.
What made him heartbroken for a time was the
unhappy feeling which sprang up between the
Serampore Triad and the Committee at home,
after Fuller died.

The sad fact was that the Committee at home
did not seem to trust Carey and Marshman and
Ward as they should. They complained about the
money they spent—those three who were living
on a pittance, and paying practically everything
they earned into the Mission! I suppose really it
was a case of good, honest, stubborn Christian
men in England misunderstanding good, honest

Christian men in India. It was a sad story, but Carey never bore malice, so neither will we.

In some ways it was understandable. These good men on the Committee were receiving generous gifts every day of the week for the work of the Mission. People sent their pennies, their sixpences, shillings, florins, half-crowns, crowns, sovereigns, guineas, and even larger sums: and it was the Committee's bounden duty to see that it was spent wisely on behalf of the givers.

What they quite overlooked was that Carey and Marshman and Ward were themselves givers, not receivers.

In the end Ward went to England to try to straighten things out: but with little result. And he died in 1823. Marshman went to England in 1827, but though he found some of the Committee friendly, some were still hopelessly prejudiced. The trouble was that by this time, none of the people on the Committee knew the Triad. They only knew the younger missionaries, many of whom did not get on too well with schoolmaster Marshman, though they had nothing to say against Carey.

But Carey and Marshman were the last people on earth to make mischief; and rather than cause a split they finally agreed to make over to the Baptist Missionary Society everything which had been under their control in the Serampore family.

It was with sad hearts that they took the printing press and their personal belongings away, and settled down in the College. Yet the sorrow passed, and Carey spent several more long, happy, useful years there.

It was a wrench when government orders compelled him to retire from the Fort William College after thirty years. But soon he was taking more and more classes in the Serampore College, and his translation work had no end to it.

Even when he was nearly seventy he was up so early in the morning for his routine ride of four or five miles, that he was back at home ready to begin translation before sunrise: and as Marshman wrote, he was "as cheerful and happy as the day is long."

But Carey's task was nearly finished. He could look at the state of the work in India with a joyous and thankful heart: he himself said that he had "scarcely a wish ungratified." His Bengali Bible had once more been revised—the Old Testament for the third time, and the New Testament for the eighth. The College was firmly established on a foundation which the years have left unshaken. The schools were thriving, and never had the Mission had so many stations, covering such a wide area.

His two younger sons William and Jabez were with him in Serampore: and Jonathan—the one who had been born while Carey was waiting to sail to India—was the Mission's Indian treasurer.

Carey grew weary: he had passed through so many trials, weathered so many storms. And although he took little account of it—and neither have we—he suffered from repeated attacks of fever during the past years.

His joy in his garden was undying: when he was not strong enough to walk there, he was taken round in a kind of Heath Robinson bath chair, made by sitting an ordinary chair on a little wooden platform with four wheels. And when even that was too much for him, the gardener would come to his room to tell him how this plant, or that tree or shrub, was getting on.

He still had a lively sense of fun. One day as Marshman was going out of the room, leaving Carey with the doctor, he said to him:

"Why so sad, Carey?"

Carey hadn't realised that he was looking sad. He certainly didn't as he said to the doctor, with a twinkle in his eye:

"After I am gone *Brother Marshman will turn the cows into my garden!*"

Brother Marshman did not. For years, until the land was sold, he kept it all in perfect order, at his own expense.

One of the last people to speak with William Carey was Alexander Duff, a young Scotsman who landed in Bengal in 1830. Carey was seventy-three, and nearly ready to go away from this world. They talked little, but before Duff left Carey whispered, *"Pray!"* Duff knelt down by the bed, and prayed; and then he said "Goodnight," and turned to go.

"Mr. Duff," called Carey faintly, as the

young Scotsman reached the door: Duff had to strain his ears to hear:

"Mr. Duff, you have been speaking about Doctor Carey, Doctor Carey . . . When I am gone say nothing about Doctor Carey . . . *Speak about Doctor Carey's Saviour!*"

And here we are, more than a hundred years later, still busy disobeying Doctor Carey's dying request to the tune of some twenty-two thousand words. And we make no apology for it. Doctor Carey used to call himself a plodder: we think he was a grand man of God, and something of a hero.